Leadership Lessons Learned in Dog Obedience School

© caraman - Fotolia.com

Douglas Young

Cover design by Caraman – Fotolia.com

First Printing: July 2009

Second Printing: December 2017

ISBN Number:1981403094

EAN-13: 9781981403097

Printed in the United States of America.

"There are times when even the best manager is like the little boy with the big dog waiting to see where the dog wants to go so he can take him there."

Lee Iacocca, US auto business executive

"In order to really enjoy a dog, one doesn't merely try to train him to be semi-human. The point of it is to open oneself to the possibility of becoming partly a dog."

Edward Hoagland

I've seen a look in dogs' eyes, a quickly vanishing look of amazed contempt, and I am convinced that basically, dogs think humans are nuts."

John Steinbeck

Dedicated to

Montgomery, a Bedlington Terrier, who came to me as if by destiny. He taught me the meaning of unconditional love and changed my views on dog training for all time.

The **Dandies Dinmont Terriers** who rule my life, and who teach me new lessons every day.

Amir – in the end there can only be one

Contents

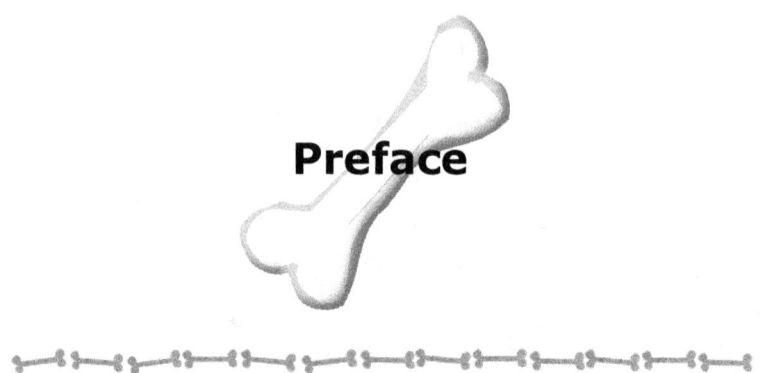

Preface

My life with dogs started with a poodle when I was around 13. Suki was my first dog and kindled in me a love for dogs that has remained with me throughout my life. In 1970, I purchased my first show dog, a Bedlington Terrier I named Montgomery. Such an amazing animal.

Besides introducing me to the sport of dog showing, he was my first obedience dog. He taught me more than I taught him. Because of Montgomery, I met my first Dandie Dinmont Terrier, and that encounter has resulted in me owning the breed for over four decades.

I took my first obedience dog-training course in 1974. The methods used at that time would seem harsh by today's standards, though they were very effective. To train your dog effectively required lightning-quick reflexes. Choke collars could actually become "collars that choked" if you didn't do things correctly. Training moved at a quick pace, and you had to be "on your toes" to get good results.

We are not talking about being abusive; it's just that training was done differently then. I attended every dog-training clinic I could and learned important lessons from some of the finest trainers of that period. These people are still talked about today, and their books remain required reading.

One such personality was Captain Haggerty from the Bronx, New York. At a clinic he presented in Cincinnati, Ohio, he not only inspired us with his knowledge and enthusiasm, but he said something I never forgot. In trying to get us to understand the role we play in the lives of our dogs, he said, *"Dogs are the only animals that can see their God. Never forget that"*. I never have.

From these seminars, as well as from reading numerous training books, I learned how important it was to communicate your desires to the dog in a way *the dog* would understand. I learned how to redirect inappropriate behavior correctly. I learned how important it was to praise the dog immediately when it did what you were asking it to do.

It wasn't long before I started training others in basic dog obedience. Many of the students could not master the training techniques I was trying to teach them, so I began looking for alternative ways of helping them train their dogs. Easier ways. Ways that made the training fun for both the dog and owner. The techniques I employed are commonly used today by many dog-training centers. And with them, both the dog and the trainer prospered.

When you live and work with dogs, your education never ends. For me, that "education" took a new direction in 2003 with the addition of alpacas and working livestock guardian dogs to our mini-farm. Alpacas are fairly defenseless unless you consider making high-pitched sounds a form of defense. We don't, and neither would any predator intent on selecting one for its dinner. To protect the alpacas, we introduced Anatolian Shepherds to our operation.

Living with the Anatolians has been a remarkable experience. Training them to be effective guardians is quite different from training an obedience dog. For the most part, you correct inappropriate behaviors, and they do the rest. It's a bit more complicated than that, but true working dogs will amaze you with their intelligence. If you are paying attention, they will try to show you the proper way to protect their charges.

Predators take one look at these magnificent dogs and move on to easier pickings.

 From a professional standpoint, I started teaching people skills to people somewhere around 1980. I created and instructed programs on topics such as interpersonal communication skills, creative problem solving, customer service, time management and leadership development. I've presented a variety of other workshops, and have made presentations at numerous conferences.

Without realizing it, I was traveling two parallel paths when it came to the training I was providing. I was training people to train their dogs, and training people to lead other people.

Regardless of the "*student*," the same topics were being covered. Both types of student:

- Needed to communicate effectively
- Needed to understand personality styles
- Needed to understand the importance of setting high, but achievable, goals and objectives, and
- So much more

In the mid-1990's, while looking for a different way to present seminars on leadership skills, it dawned on me that the training concepts and techniques I was teaching to people who were working with their dogs were *exactly* the same things being taught to people who aspired to be effective leaders. The similarities were remarkable.

A new workshop was born, and this book is the result of the lessons in leadership one can learn in dog obedience school. Going to the dogs now has a new meaning. It means you can become a more effective leader of people by learning how to lead a dog!

Treating your employees as if they were dogs may not be such a bad thing!

Doug Young

Chapter 1

Introduction

Author's note to reader: *Throughout this book, you may freely substitute the word "employee" for the words "dog" and "student," and the word "leader" for "trainer." Whatever the topic or situation being described, the message will remain valid.*

Communication, teamwork, respect, motivation, understanding personalities, rewarding an outstanding performance. Read any book, or attend any seminar, on "How to be an Effective Leader" and these are the topics most likely to be addressed.

Communication, teamwork, respect, motivation, understanding personalities, rewarding an outstanding performance. Enroll in a dog obedience training class, and these are the topics that are covered.

Coincidence? Not at all. If you have ever had the opportunity to observe a well-trained obedience dog go through its paces, you were observing the finest elements of leadership in action.

The outstanding performance turned in by the dog was the result of hours of instruction, guidance and mentoring provided by the dog's trainer. It did not happen by chance or luck. Through actions and behaviors, the trainer demonstrated a clear understanding of the fundamental aspects of leadership, and an understanding of how and when to apply those fundamentals. The trainer did not depend on one, and only one, style of teaching; or randomly apply different training techniques in the hope that something would work.

And, what about the dog? You were watching an animal that had been properly corrected when it did something wrong, not one who was improperly corrected while trying to do the right thing. Through it all, the dog, who, by the way, was being asked to do things no self-respecting dog would voluntarily do, remained an enthusiastic "worker" eagerly tackling each new challenge. Most likely, it was wagging its tail (if it had one).

You were also watching a highly motivated student accomplish very difficult tasks with a high level of proficiency.

The dog had not been mentally abused, nor did the trainer destroy its morale or stifle its motivation. There was no name-calling or cursing. No one was made to feel like an idiot.

You were also witnessing a high level of interpersonal communication. Important information was not withheld.

No "can you guess what I want you to do next" games were being played.

You observed teamwork, participatory management, and motivational techniques woven into one cohesive and outstanding performance.

People who sign up to take a dog training class might think they are merely becoming involved in a fun and worthwhile activity with their dog. In actuality, they are learning, with some minor modifications, the basics of Situational Leadership®, a model of leadership co-developed in 1969 by Dr. Paul Hersey and Dr. Ken Blanchard. This leadership "model" has become the basis of the most prevalent leadership system in the world. It works with dogs as well as it works with people.

Maybe if we try to think like a dog and consider what it would take for us to become an outstanding performer in the obedience ring, we would be better prepared to lead people.

If you ever have the opportunity to work for someone who is well versed in the art of dog obedience training, my recommendation would be to work for that person. You would indeed be lucky if they treated you as they treat their dog.

There is one other observation worth keeping in mind. After years of observation, clearly "lessons learned" do not always translate into "lessons applied." We all know people who talk a good game, but it is obvious from their actions and behaviors they are the ones who should be at the other end of the leash.

Chapter 2

Bark to School

Numerous books have been published containing the "leadership secrets" of a diverse group of people – some real, some fictional. For example, you can learn leadership secrets from the likes of:

- Abraham Lincoln[1]
- Attila the Hun[2]
- Jean Luc Picard – Captain of the Starship Enterprise[3]
- Santa Claus[4]
- General George Patton[5]

---

[1] Don T. Phillips, *Lincoln on Leadership: executive strategies for tough times* (New York: Warner Books, 1993)

[2] Wess Roberts, *Leadership Secrets of Attila the Hun* (New York: Warner Books, 1990)

[3] Wes Roberts and Bill Ross, *Make It So (Star Trek: The Next Generation)* (New York: Pocket Books, 1995)

[4] Eric Harvey, David Cottrell, and Al Lucia, *Leadership Secrets of Santa Claus* (Sept 2004)

[5] Alan Axelrod, *Patton on Leadership* (New Jersey: Prentice Hall Press, 1999)

Or, you can gain valuable insights about leadership techniques and strategies by understanding what it takes to lead a Navy SEAL team[6], or a squad of US Army Elite Rangers[7].

You can learn effective leadership skills from a mouse (or should I say *The Mouse*[8]), the Bible[9], a never-ending list of sports coaches and politicians or even from spending time as a Benedictine Monk[10].

However, after reading these books, it struck me that something was missing from these resources. While it is true you will glean useful information from the pages of these books, how does someone who has never served as a US Army Ranger or a Navy Seal apply *those* lessons to what goes on in the everyday work world? Further, few of us will ever become a Benedictine Monk, captain a Starship, or coach a sports team.

---

6 Jeff Cannon and Jon Cannon *Leadership Lessons of the Navy SEALS : Battle-Tested Strategies for Creating Successful Organizations and Inspiring Extraordinary Results* (McGraw-Hill, 2004)

7 Brace E. Barber, *No Excuse Leadership: Lessons from the U.S. Army's Elite Rangers* (New Jersey: John Wiley and Sons, Inc., 2004)

8 Bill Capodagli and Lynn Jackson, *The Disney Way: Harnessing the Management Secrets of Disney in Your Company,* (New York, McGraw Hill, 1999}

9 Laurie Beth Jones, *Jesus CEO: Using Ancient Wisdom for Visionary Leadership,* (Hyperion, April 18, 1996)

10 James C. Hunter, *The Servant: A Simple Story About the True Essence of Leadership* (Roseville, CA: Prima Publishing, 1998)

Most of us will never have the opportunity to sit down over a cup of coffee and discuss leadership skills with these individuals. While doing so would be nice, it would be difficult to set up a meeting as many of them are either dead, or they simply do not exist.

So, if an opportunity to meet in person with these people is not a possibility, and since we can't re-live the experiences that helped shape their leadership skills, how and where can you learn to become a more effective leader?

Based on years of observation and first-hand experience, I would argue that the best, but most overlooked place to learn how to be an effective leader is **Dog Obedience School.**

 ***Dog Obedience School?*** "How so," you might ask. Since the mid-1990's, I have instructed numerous dog obedience-training classes. Hundreds of people have entrusted me to train them so that they could train their dogs.

What I observed was that anyone could train a dog provided they worked at it and did not give up early in the process. Some people were better at it than others, but anyone who tried enjoyed a measure of success. What I realized, but the dog trainers were probably unaware of it, was that while *they* were learning how to help their dogs become better citizens, they were also learning valuable lessons about leading people.

Obedience school is the perfect environment to learn effective leadership skills while putting them into practice.

You can apply the lessons being taught in real time, providing you with immediate feedback. You can practice them until you get them right. Moreover, if you make a mistake, you can try again with a student that will forgive you for your blunders a lot more easily than a person ever would.

Just ask an obedience school graduate *(dog or human)*, and I am sure they will agree. Thousands of dogs, whose owners were smart enough to enroll them in a dog training class, can testify to the benefits of this type of training and this type of learning. And, if asked, I am sure they would tell you that life is more pleasant living with a knowledgeable, skilled trainer, then with an uninformed, clueless one.

Chapter 3

Sit... Stay... Come... Down. Good Dog!

Before reading further, take a moment to answer the following questions:

Question #1: Have you ever owned a dog or do you own one now?

Actually, your answer does not matter. Even if you have never owned a dog, you can still benefit from the lessons covered in this book. Your answer to question #2 is more important and may reveal more about you than you care to admit.

Question #2: Are you owned by a cat?

If you answered "Yes" to question #2, nothing in this book will be of value to you. The purpose of this book is to generate an appreciation for the leadership lessons learned in dog obedience school so you can apply them to leading people. Think for a moment, how many cat-training centers are there? To underscore this point, you can turn to Chapter 16 where I've listed <u>all</u> of the known *Leadership Lessons Learned in Cat Obedience school.*

Let's continue with a few more questions.

Question #3: Is your dog an obedient pet?

Question #4: Does your relationship with your dog live up to your expectations of the "ownership experience"?

Question #5: Is the relationship one that will create great sadness when it ends?

If you answered "yes" to any of these questions you would probably agree with the statement: *"relationships with dogs can be pleasant, fun, and rewarding."*

However, in some instances, these relationships can become something to dread. You do not need to be a dog owner to know what it means to have a poorly trained pet. The untrained, undisciplined rogue of a dog is nobody's idea of a fun companion.

Train 'Em While They're Young!

Puppies are like an empty vessel. What they are filled up with molds them into the type of companion they will become. We probably all know of a cute, innocent puppy that, because it did not receive proper guidance and direction, grew up to become an uncontrollable *beast!*

With that thought in mind, allow me to pose three additional questions for those readers whose dog ownership experiences have been less than perfect.

Question #6: Does your relationship with your dog leave something to be desired?

Question #7: Are your expectations, on everything from performance to housebreaking, different from your reality?

Questions #8: Is it fair to say the dog has turned on you? Possibly even bit the hand that feeds it?

I hope that this has not been your experience, but if it has, take some solace in that you are not alone. Such situations do occur.

While relationships with dogs can be fun and rewarding, they can also be disappointing and full of surprises. When

our expectations are not met, we might ask "How and why did this happen?" and "Could anything have been done to prevent it from happening?" The answers are not always easy, but perhaps a little "leash training" (see Chapter 8) could have helped.

You may have noticed it is not very different with people. Try replacing the word "dog" with "employee" and rereading questions 6 through 8. *(Most of us do not have to worry about housebreaking employees, or at least I hope not).* You can probably identify at least one person who prompts you to answer, "Yes, yes, and yes"!

Like a puppy, new employees can be considered an empty vessel. What they are filled up with molds them into the type of employee they become. When they enter the workforce, they are full of hopes, dreams and aspirations. Like the untrained puppy, they are motivated and enthusiastic, but directionless.

One thing they are not is stupid. With proper guidance and direction, they will "grow." Great things will be achieved.

However, without proper guidance and direction, one day, like the puppy who grows to become 85 lbs of out-of-control mayhem, the employee evolves into the equivalent of the *beast puppy!*

Off to the Dog Pound

What do dog owners do when they feel they can no longer live with their dog? They may do any number of things – some worse than others. They may abandon it to a dog house located at the furthest reaches of their property, try to give it away to some unsuspecting

person or dump it at a dog shelter (or worse).

And, what do managers do when they realize they have an employee they can no longer work with? They may do any number of things – some worse than others. They may abandon the employee to a desk in a remote part of the office, promote or transfer him to some other unsuspecting manager or dump him off at a dog shelter – whoops, skip that idea. While it would be nice, shelters have enough to worry about without having to deal with discarded employees.

Over the years, associates who I have worked with in the Human Resources field have said they would classify 3% – 4% of the workforce as "problem employees." Sure,  there are employees who may challenge you in many different ways, but they are not the "hardcore cases." This small percentage of individuals represents those people where nothing seems to work. Why they behave the way they do is often a mystery. They seem to think they can do whatever they want and that rules and regulations were meant only for others.

Dogs also fit this description with a very small percentage of them being described as "hardcore cases." Like their human counterparts, they seem to think they can do whatever they want and that rules and regulations were created for others.

Fortunately, these people (and these dogs) are rare. We probably all know of at least one person who believes their sole purpose in life is to go to work to create problems rather than putting their energy into helping to prevent or resolve problems. The majority of people do not get up every morning wondering what they can do to make everyone (including themselves) miserable. Most people prefer doing the *right thing* the *right way*.

But, for those people who want to do the right thing the right way, what usually happens when they arrive at work? They do not receive the training they need to be successful. Their input and ideas are ignored. They are treated with little or no respect, and a "job-well-done" is not noticed or appreciated.

Like the dog that avoids its owner so as not to be kicked, people avoid doing routine tasks and stop taking risks because they also want to avoid being kicked. No wonder so many people turn on their managers.

Early training, done correctly, can spell the difference between a dog that becomes a close family member and one that spends its life isolated from its humans. The dog owner who understands how to teach, mold and reinforce desired behaviors will reap the rewards of a life-long companion.

Early training, done correctly, can also spell the difference between the employee who is considered a valuable asset and one that spends his life isolated from his coworkers. The supervisor who understands how to teach, mold and reinforce desired behaviors will reap the results of a motivated, productive workforce.

Remember this *when managers treat their people like dogs, they had best be prepared to be bitten!*

© caraman - Fotolia.com

Chapter 4

Dogs Are Different From People
(If Only Slightly)

To this point, it might appear as if I consider dogs and people to be equals. So please let me assure the reader I recognize they are two separate species. Dogs do not think as we do, nor do we have to worry about them taking over *most* of our jobs. Unfortunately, far too many managers treat their employees like dogs. In fact, many of us treat our dogs better than some managers treat their employees.

Managers who do not want to take the time to learn how to mold people into outstanding performers might be better off with a staff of dogs. The dog has many attributes that would qualify it as *the* model employee.

The Dog - The Model Employee

To begin with, unlike many people, dogs have been domesticated for thousands of years. They easily understand who their boss is. They will work for an occasional pat on the head. Toss them a biscuit or a bone, and they will consider themselves aptly rewarded and think you are wonderful. With little encouragement, they enthusiastically go about their business. They ask for little but give a lot.

And, if need be, they can be put in a cage to give their owners some rest. Cage training is a highly recommended practice – for a dog. It is a safe and secure environment, usually equipped with a big, fluffy, bed. The cage often becomes a refuge for the dog, a personal fortress of solitude.

Humans share a similar environment with some minor modifications. Employees call their cages "cubicles." While cubicles have some of the qualities of a dog cage, they are not as effective (or as comfortable). They do not come with big fluffy beds, nor do they have doors that can be latched shut, though that might be a useful feature.

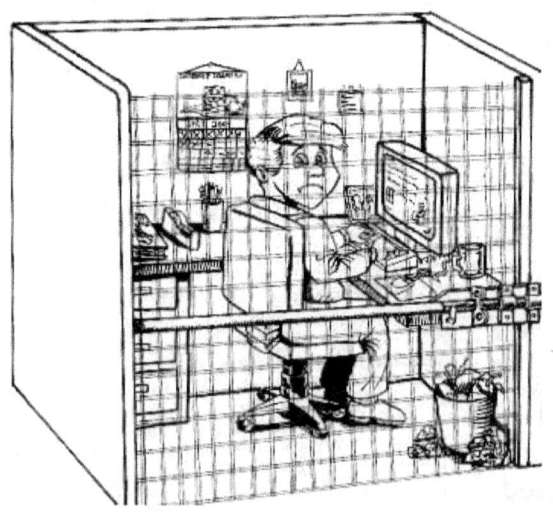

Also, if you are a dog you know it is OK to go to into your cage and take a nap. Unfortunately, cubicles can have the same effect on people.

As much as some managers might like the idea, "caging" employees, even for limited amounts of time, is frowned upon.

Ironically, while dogs might be better employees than most people, they do exhibit some similar reactions when mistreated. If backed into a corner or if abused, they can fight back. We read where "dog bites man." We also read where "employee shoots boss."

When Good Dogs Go Bad

When someone is having trouble with their dog, they often enroll it in an obedience training class. The expectation is that somehow the "*class*" will miraculously solve all of their dog's problems.

They quickly learn that a dog obedience class is not designed to train their dog *for them*. What they discover is that the objective of the class is to train *them* so they can train *their* dog.

This is an important distinction. In one instance, they were expecting someone else to solve their problems for them. In the second instance, they are learning to solve their problems for themselves.

Boot Camp for Dogs

Learning to be an effective leader for your dog is quite different than sending your dog away to be trained by someone else. Having some-one else train your dog is like sending your kid to military school for a few years. Let  someone else deal with the kid and, ideally, when he comes back he will be a model citizen.

The problem with this approach is that while the dog may be learning new things, you are not. The dog's trainer may work with you to help you understand what you need to do to reinforce what *he* or *she* has been doing. However, this approach is not a substitute for personal involvement and improvement.

Most managers probably wish there was something equivalent to "dog obedience school" for problem employees, except they might want to call it a more politically correct name like "*Employee Motivation and Cooperation School.*" Wouldn't that be nice?

While they may wish for such a "school," many managers already engage in a practice similar in concept. A common management solution for dealing with a poor performer is to send the individual to a training program to improve their attitude or effectiveness. Usually, this happens because the manager doesn't know what else to do.

The same concern is raised here as was raised about sending a dog to someone else for training. While the employee may be learning new things, the manager's skills do not improve. Seminar leaders do not make it a habit of sitting down with an attendee's supervisor to provide guidance on how to reinforce the training that has been received.

Dog Trainers – Are They Born or Made?

Why are some people better dog trainers than others? Why are some people better leaders than others? Leader of people – leader of dogs – are they really any different? In either case, where do these people come from? Are they born with the knowledge to lead, or is it learned?

I do not believe we are born with some innate ability to train a dog any more than we are born with the skills or knowledge necessary to enable us to lead people effectively. Anyone who takes his/her learning seriously can become an effective leader of (*insert name of what it is you want to lead.*)

Learning is the key to success. This is not some big, dark secret shared by only a few. While some people may wish to debate the question of whether leaders are born or made, there is little disagreement that leadership skills can be mastered by anyone who puts forth the effort.

If we hope to be successful, we should be willing to learn new ways to look at and do things if we hope to be successful in establishing and building the kind of relationships we desire. It doesn't matter whether we are talking about dogs or people.

Chapter 5

Choosing a Leader of the Pack

How often are new supervisors selected based solely on seniority? Many people may apply for a supervisory position, but it often comes down to who has been employed the longest that settles the question of who is most qualified *to lead*.

Decisions of this type are made a little differently in the canine world. If they were not, things could get interesting. Perhaps we could learn something from the wolf, cousin to the dog.

Imagine for a moment that you are a wolf cub. What fun. All day long you get to do "wolfie" things, such as chasing down dinner, frolicking with your friends, drinking from streams and marking your territory.

As you grow up, if you are a smart wolf, you observe the behavior of the pack leader. You learn what it takes to earn the respect of the rest of the pack. You learn how to create order and provide for your family.

As part of the cycle of life, one day the leader of the pack passes on. If you've learned your lessons well, you may find that the rest of the pack turns to you for direction and guidance. Sure, there may be some growling and snarling from others who think they are more qualified, but because you know how to lead, you are chosen to lead.

Now consider this scenario. Imagine for a moment you are a wolf cub. What fun. All day long you get to do "wolfie" things, such as chasing down dinner, frolicking with your friends, drinking from streams and marking your territory. (Sound familiar).

Except this time around, you are having too much fun. You certainly do not have time to observe the pack leader and, so, you learn nothing about leadership.

 Time passes. One day the leader of the pack passes on. Everyone looks around, and someone starts checking the personnel files. The records show you have been in the pack the longest. You have seniority. That means you *must* be qualified to lead. Congratulations, the promotion is yours. So, now you have an entire pack of wolves, all with really sharp teeth, looking at you and saying "O.K., lead us". And, under their breath, I am sure they are saying, "If you can."

Now, consider those individuals who go from being just one of the guys (a member of the pack) to a position of leadership (the new pack leader). Like the wolf who was not paying attention, how prepared are these people to lead?

If they spent their time chasing down their next meal, frolicking with their friends, drinking from the water cooler and marking (err, protecting) their territory, they are probably no more prepared to lead than the wolf who goofed off. And, the people they are supposed to lead will probably eat them alive!

How can you prepare yourself for leadership opportunities? There are many ways. Go to your local library or bookstore and chose from an amazing array of books. Read the books, don't just pile them on your desk to impress others. View videos. Research the subject on the Internet. Attend seminars and workshops. Watch and learn from people you respect. Watch and learn from people you do _not_ respect. It doesn't matter how you choose to expand your knowledge and understanding, as long as you do something!

And, of course, I would be remiss if I didn't recommend that you enroll your dog in an obedience training class and gain first-hand experience of the techniques and ideas discussed in this book.

Chapter 6

Starting Out on the Right Paw

A typical dog obedience class usually takes 6 - 8 weeks to complete. New lessons are introduced weekly, and by the end of the program, the trainers will have been exposed to a great deal of information. If they learn their lessons well, and they apply those lessons correctly, their dogs will have shown great improvement and will be well on their way to becoming model citizens.

For those readers who have never taken a dog through a training course, it might be helpful to know that five exercises are taught in an introductory program. The first of these is heeling, which teaches control and requires the dog's undivided attention. When heeling, the dog walks alongside the trainer without being dragged or without tugging on its leash. When the trainer comes to a stop, the dog automatically sits parallel to the trainer's left leg and waits for the next set of instructions.

The dog also learns the "sit and stay," the "down and stay," the "stand-for-examination" and the "recall" or come exercise.

Beyond basic obedience, the exercises build in complexity. In advanced classes, the dog is introduced to retrieving objects, jumping over barriers, working without a leash and responding to hand signals.

New Employee Orientation

The first training class is no different than the first day on a new job or in a new position. Consider it the equivalent of new employee orientation.

A well-developed and thought-out employee orientation program should have two phases. All too often, there is only one phase, and it generally receives little attention. It lasts maybe a day and consists of letting the new employee know where their desk, and the nearest restroom, is located.

Not all companies share this view, and that is a welcomed approach. These companies employ a two-phase approach to orientation. Phase 1 is the actual "orientation phase," and spans the first day through the first week of employment. The primary focus is on setting expectations and explaining goals and objectives. It is also when the employee learns where their desk, and the restrooms, are located.

Phase 2 is an extended training phase and might last as long as six months to a year. It is during this time that organizations take steps to integrate the employee into the culture and philosophy of how work is done in the organization.

Take a dog training class, and you will not only experience such an orientation process, but you will see how effective it can be. Phase 1 equates to the first class. It is here trainers receive information on what they will be teaching their dogs. This class covers such topics as:

- How to communicate with your dog
- How and when to praise
- How and when to correct
- The proper use of the leash and collar

It also covers the philosophy of training to be used and the importance of setting high, but achievable objectives. It is here where some of the *most important* lessons are learned.

The next five to seven sessions consist of applying those lessons to teaching the dog how to do what we want the dog to do. This is the equivalent of Phase 2 of the orientation phase. It is the "extended training phase."

In some dog training classes, instructors seem impatient to get the people and their dogs onto the training floor with little or no orientation! They then try to instruct the class in the midst of mass confusion.

When instructing a dog obedience class, I avoided dragging the handlers and their dogs onto the training floor during the first session. I believed the best way to go about the learning process was to build a strong foundation upon which all subsequent learning is based. That cannot be done with the dogs lunging at one another, or with the trainers' attention diverted as they try to control their dogs. Therefore, it is critical that the dog owners be orientated properly before proceeding further.

Providing the novice trainer with a well-designed orientation program provides immediate benefits. Because the trainers are not distracted, it gives them an opportunity to learn. The results are evident in how they interact with their dogs, and how rapidly both the dogs and the trainers progress.

This approach also works extremely well with people. People deserve the same opportunity to start a new job or a new challenge on a firm foundation - one that gives them a chance to grow. They also deserve a well-thought-out "extended training phase" so their success is assured.

I never believed in throwing new employees "to the wolves" without making sure they knew what to expect, or what was expected from them. To do so was an open invitation for failure.

Dog trainers understand the importance of a *"new dog orientation program."* They know a well-conceived plan will lead them and their dog in the right direction. Such a process is essential to achieving their goals and objectives. People could benefit from this lesson.

The 1st Leadership Lesson Learned in Dog Obedience School

The first training class is no different than the first day on a new job or in a new position. Each subsequent class is designed to further enhance the dog's performance. When combined together, all the classes can be considered the equivalent of a new employee orientation program.

It is an opportunity to develop a firm foundation upon which all subsequent growth is based. It helps avoid mass confusion and sets the stage for future growth and development.

It is more than showing the dog where the nearest (tree) restroom is. A well-designed orientation program:

- Provides an opportunity to set expectations, explain work goals and objectives and set performance standards, and
- It has an extended training phase, during which people are integrated into the culture and philosophy of how work is done in the organization.

Chapter 7

The "Ring Wise" Employee

Dogs learn in black and white. When performing an exercise, as far as a dog is concerned, there are only two ways to do it:

- The right way, and
- The wrong way.

While there may be many ways to do an exercise *wrong*, there is only one way to do it *right*. If a dog is shown what it is supposed to do and is not allowed to do it any other way, it will learn to do the task correctly. Obviously, this requires the trainer to be consistent in his or her training methodology. It's not fair to the dog to require it do an exercise one way today, and allow it to do it differently (or incorrectly) the next time. That just confuses the poor animal.

There is a lesson here for how we should train people to do their jobs. All too often, they are not properly prepared, and the results are predictable. If people don't know what to do, or how to do it, how can they be expected to do it correctly?

When people don't know how to do properly complete a task, they can get pretty creative. Of course, sometimes the problem is that they *don't* want to do what they are supposed to do. When that's the case, we *really* learn how creative they can be in avoiding work.

Where people are concerned, there are times when creativity is a good thing. After all, if they never explored new ways to do things, they would never find better ways to do things.

Dogs can also get creative at times. However, there is a difference. In the obedience ring, what we require a dog to do is usually much more structured than what we normally ask a person to do. There isn't much reason for a dog to seek out new or better ways to do a particular exercise. Generally speaking, dogs are not big when it comes to "process improvement."

However, trainers occasionally run into the "creative dog," and when they do, they have to learn to deal with such an animal. We have a term for these dogs; we say they are "ring wise." Let me explain what that term means.

How to Earn an AKC Obedience Degree

Training takes place inside a "ring," an area bounded by ropes or gates that delineates the work area. The ring size is determined by American Kennel Club (AKC) rules. If a dog leaves the ring during a practice session, it will receive an appropriate correction. However, if the dog is competing to earn an AKC obedience degree, and it leaves the ring at an obedience trial, it will be disqualified for that day's event (and no biscuits or other treats that day!)

To earn an AKC obedience degree, the team of handler and dog will enter obedience trials. They compete at one of three levels. Those levels are:

Novice: For the dog just getting started in obedience.

Open: The second level that includes exercises that are more complicated.

Utility: The third and highest level of obedience competition.

At each trial, depending on the level of competition they are competing at, they will execute from five to seven specific exercises. They are evaluated on how accurately they complete each exercise. A perfect score is 200 points, with a minimum of 170 points required to qualify. To gain their obedience degree, they will have to qualify three times by attending three different trials under the watchful eye of two different judges.

The handler and/or dog lose points if they fail to do something correctly. Further, each exercise is judged independently. If any exercise receives a failing grade (less than 50% of the points for each exercise), the team will not qualify even if they flawlessly complete all the other exercises.

When all of the teams at a particular level have completed their exercises, the scores are tabulated, and ribbons are distributed for 1st through 4th place. Winning your class is a proud achievement, and can only be accomplished if the dog and handler work together as a team.

At the end of the day, when all the scores have been tabulated for *all* of the teams, regardless of the level they were competing at, the team with the highest score is awarded the coveted **High In Trial** award.

High in Trial Award

The Ring Wise Employee (Dog)

When in the ring, it is amazing what some dogs will try to get away with. During a practice session, they know their trainer can, and will, redirect any inappropriate behaviors or actions. Therefore, they might turn in a great performance under those conditions.

What drives trainers nuts is how quickly their dogs figure out they *cannot be corrected* in front of a judge or any spectators. They will look their trainer in the eye, and do whatever they want to do. We refer to these dogs as being "ring-wise."

Every trainer has observed the "ring-wise" dog. It is not something you easily forget. While I could provide a number of examples of this behavior, one performance in particular sticks in my memory. The dog in question was well known to me, and she was a steady worker. She knew *how* to do what she was *supposed* to do. Nevertheless, on this particular day, none of that mattered.

During the heeling phase of the routine, she left her trainer's side to check on all the interesting items under a table set-up alongside the ring. She even stuck her nose in the judge's handbag. Looking up, she noticed that her handler, who had continued to walk along as required, was 20 feet away. The dog quickly caught up to her with the most innocent look on her face.

During the down-stay exercise, she again demonstrated she was going to test how serious everyone was about this "competition thing." The "down-stay" exercise requires the trainer to place the dog in the "Down" position and command it to "Stay." The handler walks some distance away, and the dog is supposed to stay where placed for three minutes without moving.

Much to the chagrin of the trainer, and the amusement of everyone but the judge, the dog, after about one minute, began crawling forward on all fours towards her owner. As she crawled, she kept one eye on the judge and one eye on her owner. She didn't rise up from the down position until she was past the judge, after which she sprinted to her owner. It was clear to everyone watching that the dog knew exactly what she was doing. She knew the job she was supposed to do, after all, she stayed in the down position while sneaking past the judge. However, she also knew she wanted her "mom," and she knew she would not be reprimanded in the ring. This was one very "ring-wise" dog. Sometimes, they are too clever for their own good.

It is important to keep in mind that she was not looking for a *better* way to do these tasks. What she was doing was "testing" *her* trainer to see how serious *she* was about her doing the job.

Is it any different with people? Of course not. Leaders would be well advised to watch for signs they are dealing with a "ring-wise employee." Such an individual knows how and what they are supposed to do. They just don't want to do it! When this happens, we are dealing with a "performance problem." Unfortunately, most managers see it, and treat it, as a "training problem." To be an effective leader, we need the ability to differentiate between these two types of problems.

Problems come in many different forms. For example:

- The employee was never properly trained in the first place.
- The task hasn't been done in a while, and the employee needs a refresher.
- The work had changed, and the employee needs new or updated information on how to complete the task.

With proper guidance, these problems are easily resolved. The trick is identifying that the problem is, indeed, a training problem.

In many instances, managers simply don't think or attempt to analyze why a problem exists. Their response to an employee's behavior is to threaten or reprimand them when a guiding hand might be more appropriate.

Dog trainers are constantly making decisions of this type. It's part of *their* training! It's what makes the best trainers so successful. Leaders would benefit tremendously if they developed the skills to recognize when they were in the presence of a "performance problem" or a "training problem."

Anyone in a leadership position could benefit from reading *Why Employees Don't Do What They're Supposed To Do and What To Do About It,* by Ferdinand F. Fournies. Fournies addresses, in an easy to understand format, the many reasons why employees fail to do what they are supposed to do and provides specific actions managers can take to improve employee productivity.

Fournies outlines a number of reasons why people don't do what they are expected to do. Listed below are ten of them. When a person (or a dog) fails to perform as desired, any one of these reasons may explain "Why?" Note that some of these reasons are "training issues" and some are "performance issues." Can you tell the difference?

- They don't know why they should do it
- They don't know how to do it
- They don't know what they are supposed to do
- They think your way will not work
- They think their way is better
- They think something else is more important
- They think they are doing it
- They are punished for doing it
- They are rewarded for not doing it
- It's beyond their personal abilities

I'm not going to tell you which is which. Read Fournies book! Just understand that there is a difference between problems created due to a lack of training and problems created because of poor performance.

In the workplace, an understanding of these differences seems to be rare. In the dog trainer's world, understanding the differences is part of their everyday approach to working with their dog. It doesn't seem fair to people, does it?

Astute leaders know performance problems can be attributed to "ring wise employees"; that the employees are actually testing them to see how serious they are about the employees doing the jobs assigned to them. How they respond to these situations separates mediocre managers from successful leaders.

The 2nd Leadership Lesson Learned in Dog Obedience School

Watch for signs you are dealing with a "ring-wise dog" or employee. Such a person knows how and what it is supposed to do. It just doesn't want to do it! It will test you on a regular basis to see how serious you are about it doing the job it is supposed to do.

Additionally, leaders must be able to differentiate between a "training problem" and a "performance problem". Knowing the difference allows you to provide an appropriate response to redirecting the undesired performance.

Chapter 8

The Proper Equipment to Getting the Job Done

The standard equipment used when training a dog consists of a collar and a lead. How they are used or misused, impacts considerably on the dog's desire to learn.

We'll begin with the lead or if you prefer, leash. Leads come in a variety of lengths. You can purchase one as short as a foot in length up to the retractable kind that allows 30 feet of "freedom." Dog trainers typically use a six-foot lead. Why? Well, there are some very practical reasons for this choice.

A one to 3-foot leash is useful when walking your dog through a crowd or for situations that require the dog to be under close control. It is not useful in training situations. Imagine having your dog tethered to a three-foot lead. With every step or move you make, the dog would receive a tug on its collar. Unless the dog was paying attention 100% of the time (and since you can't do that it's not

fair to expect the dog to do so) it would find itself being jerked one way, and then another, all day long.

Imagine if your boss put a collar on you and attached it to a three-foot lead. You would be treated no differently than the dog described in the preceding paragraph. All day long, you would be jerked left and then right. It wouldn't take you very long to resent being handled in such a manner. Dogs don't like being treated this way, and neither do people.

Long, retractable leads are handy when walking or exercising your dog. You can stand in one spot while the dog explores a wide area. Such a leash works great in an open, unrestricted environment. However, this type of lead is not recommended where there are crowds of people, numerous trees or bushes, or in situations where the dog can put itself at risk. At the very least, the *misuse* of such a lead can result in a tangled mess.

It could also result in other undesirable consequences. Consider the situation where the dog has extended the leash to its full length. From out of nowhere, another dog approaches. Here you are, with 20-30' of line extended and you have to take up the slack quickly. If you're too slow, there may be some unpleasant results.

Of course, you could always let your dog run loose. No lead and no collar. The outcome of this scenario is fairly predictable; you have **no** control.

Experience has shown that a six-foot leash offers a compromise between one that is too short and one that is too long. It provides for a limited amount of freedom while allowing the trainer to bring the dog under control quickly if necessary.

Dog trainers know if they always use a short lead, the dog will be "tied" to them. They wind up dragging the dog through the lessons they are trying to teach. The result is that, by never giving the dog any slack, it never has an opportunity to show you what it has learned.

If you don't know what your dog can do, how can you "trust" it to perform? How do you know if it is progressing? Besides, the dog quickly learns to resent being dragged everywhere.

However, allow the dog too much slack, and it can get beyond your control. If you need to "redirect an inappropriate behavior," it takes too long to "reel" the dog in. No matter has fast you do this, it is not fast enough. By the time you get to the dog to correct its behavior, the dog has no idea why it is being corrected.

Leash Control in the Workplace

Now let's apply the concept of "leash control" to the workplace. Beginning with new employees, or with people who have been promoted, effective leaders know they should initially keep these people on a short lead. They know there is much to learn and they will want to guide them through the learning process.

They also know that if they provide too little slack the employees will never "grow." They will never learn to make decisions for themselves. Therefore, the astute leader recognizes when to give them some slack. However, too much slack too soon creates problems of its own. The employees will be just beyond their control. If they are not ready for that level of freedom, they will not succeed.

Moreover, what happens if we allow them to work "off-lead" before they are ready? Dogs and people differ little in this respect. No leash means no control. The dog can run off and ignore you. They will be out there peeing on the bushes where you can't stop them. That also applies to employees (figuratively speaking, of course).

Choking off Initiative

In today's training classes it is just as common to see the dog wearing a buckle-type collar or halter as it is to see them wearing a slip collar. For illustrative purposes, we will stick with the slip collar as our collar of choice.

The slip collar, which becomes a choke collar when used improperly, can be a valuable training tool. The key words are "when used improperly." The slip collar is designed to "slip" to a loose, open, position so the dog is not choked when it is doing the right thing. Used improperly, it will do just what its other name implies – choke the dog. Many novice trainers have difficulty learning how to use this type of collar properly, so they are not used as often as they were just a few years ago.

While fitting employees with collars and leashes may not be practical, there is still a valuable lesson contained in this metaphor. Figuratively speaking, employees do wear a collar and they are attached to a leash. The leader's role in all of this is to make proper use of the imaginary leash and collar.

Keep the collar too tight, and you will turn it into a choke collar. While we are not concerned with cutting off the employee's ability to breathe, the result may seem the same to the employee as he or she slowly suffocates. Continue the pressure from day to day, and you will cut off their desire to perform. Never provide any slack and people will never be able to show you what they can do.

Dog trainers must master the art of leash control. So must leaders. The concept of leash control is just another way of teaching people how and when to apply the appropriate style of leadership that is dependent on the situation. In Chapter 13, we will explore this idea by applying the principles of Situational Leadership® to the obedience ring, a lesson easily transferable to the workplace.

The 3rd Leadership Lesson Learned in Dog Obedience School

Dogs are trained using a leash and collar. Think of employees as having imaginary ones. Dog trainers know they must master the art of leash control. So must leaders. Both must learn how and when to give their people some slack or when to reel them in.

Where dogs are concerned, their slip collars can become choke collars if used improperly. Where people are concerned, improper use of their imaginary collars can, and will, "choke" off initiative and undermine motivation.

Chapter 9

To Train Your Dog You Need To Know Your Dog

Four Abilities Productive Leaders Learn and Use

In the book, *Leadership Through People Skills*, Robert E. Lefton, Ph.D. and Victor R. Buzzotta, Ph.D., identify four sets of abilities productive leaders must learn and use. They are:

Sizing-up skills.

Effective leaders can determine why people do what they do so they can make sense of what they see. This ability provides the leader with the insight to take the appropriate action from a wide choice of possible actions.

Communication skills

The ability to communicate thoughts and ideas effectively is essential to one's success. If we lack the ability to communicate, there can be no sharing of one's vision, no opportunity to learn from others. No matter how technically competent you are, if you cannot communicate effectively, nothing will become operational.

Motivational skills

Effective leaders have an understanding of motivational theory and successfully apply the principles involved. They are also aware of the characteristics that define a motivating work environment and have the necessary skills to create such an environment.

Adaptive skills

No two people are alike. No two dogs are alike. One style of leadership cannot be used on everyone. Different situations require different responses, from dog trainers and managers alike. While leaders should treat everyone fairly, they know they cannot treat everyone equally. The effective leader is aware of this and adapts his leadership style accordingly. It's **Situational Leadership™** with a leash and collar!

Learning and applying these four skills to people is difficult enough but if you want to expand your leadership capabilities, learn and apply these skills to training a dog. Do this well, and you *will* be a better leader of people!

Let's take each of these four skills, and see how they can be applied to preparing a dog for competition in the obedience ring and how that knowledge can be translated to an office environment. In this chapter, we will explore the important skill of "sizing-up" employees, and in chapters 11 - 13, we'll examine the remaining three skills.

Westminster People Club Show

Since 1984, the Westminster Kennel Club Dog Show has been shown on TV. This broadcast has not only shown the viewing public some of the drama that occurs in the "dog show world," but has given them an opportunity to see dogs they might never see. Viewers learn a little about the different dog breeds and gain some insight into how they differ in size, shape and temperament.

Among the things people learn is that dogs are placed into one of 7 different groups, primarily based on the dog's function or purpose. For example, dogs bred to herd livestock belong to the Herding Group.

You would think it would be obvious that dogs like the large working breeds would need to be handled differently from the tiny toy breeds, but watching untrained people work with such disparate breeds tells you that they have not learned this lesson. They think *a dog is a dog is a dog*. They think you can treat them all the same.

So, let's review an obvious, but important, point. All dogs are different. They come in an amazing array of sizes and shapes. There are big dogs and little dogs. They have different personalities and behavioral characteristics. They come in assorted colors. They style their hair differently though they do dress the same.

© caraman - Fotolia.com

Because dogs are different, experienced trainers know that the first thing they need to do is to "size-up" their dogs. For example, to effectively mold and mentor their dogs, they must know:

- How it "thinks" or processes information,
- How fast a learner it is,
- How it responds to praise or corrections,
- The best way to motivate it,
- How much guidance and direction it needs, and
- How much patience they will need to guide the dog to the level of performance desired.

Now, consider people. We do not need a Westminster People Show to display the many types of people or to give "viewers" an opportunity to see people they might never see. We already know there are many different "types" of people. They come in an amazing array of sizes and shapes. There are big people and little people. They have different personalities and behavioral characteristics. They come in many different colors. About the only real difference from the dog is that people both dress *and* style their hair differently from one another.

Effective leaders of people know that to mold and mentor their followers, they must learn the same things about them as a dog trainer must know about his dog. They must know:

- How (or if) they think,
- How fast a learner they are

- How they respond to praise or correction,
- What is the best way to motivate them,
- How much guidance and direction they need; and
- How much patience will be needed to get the level of performance desired

It's a simple concept: to train your dog you need to *know* your dog. To motivate, teach, and lead it, you need the insight to recognize what works and what doesn't work. Know this and you will be able to select the most appropriate course of action from a multitude of possible actions for every situation. This philosophy is so ingrained into experienced dog trainers that they would never consider handling every dog the same.

So why do so many managers insist on using one, and only one, style of management? Well, it could be because they have never trained a dog. Or, it could be they were off frolicking with their pack members when they should have been learning how to lead.

Effective leaders use the same "training" philosophy as experienced dog trainers. Different people present different challenges. Some people need more supervision than others, some less. Some can work with minimal direction; others need constant attention.

Getting to know those you expect to lead is a necessary first step. It works as well with dogs as it does with people. Each dog presents the trainer with new challenges and opportunities. Knowing what will work and what will not work requires trainers possess excellent *"sizing-up skills"*; the first of the four abilities identified by Lefton and Buzzotta.

Dog trainers know that even though the principles of training remain constant, they cannot take one style of training and use it on every dog they encounter. To update an old phrase, "different strokes for different pets."

The 4th Leadership Lesson Learned in Dog Obedience School

Every dog is different. To train your dog you need to know your dog. To motivate, teach, and lead it you need the insight to recognize what works and what doesn't work. Know this and you will be able to select the most appropriate course of action from a multitude of possible actions for every situation. It's a lesson that works equally as well with people.

To effectively mold and mentor dogs or people, you must learn:

- How they "thinks" or processes information
- How fast a learner they are
- How they respond to praise or corrections
- The best way to motivate them
- How much guidance and direction they need
- How much patience you will need to guide either of them to the level of performance desired.

Chapter 10

Set the Bar High

Achieving a High Level of Performance

How does a dog reach the level of performance desired by its trainer while staying enthusiastic? What is the trainer's formula for success? Keep in mind that the things we ask dogs to do are not much different from what we ask people to do – while they are things they are supposed to do, they would probably not do them if left to their own devices.

It starts with the trainer's ability to understand and implement two very important concepts. First, they have to be able to grasp the big picture. They need to know what a perfect performance looks like.

Secondly, they understand that each exercise is composed of a number of steps. They know that to teach their dog a new "task," they have to break the exercise down into its individual components.

We could summarize it as follows; with an understanding of the exercise to be taught, the trainer must:

- Learn the steps involved in completing the task
- Know how long it might take the dog to learn each step
- Know how to combine the steps into one smooth operation, and throughout the entire process
- Demonstrate he knows how to motivate his dog

The result is a dog, and a trainer, who do not get frustrated. The dog learns how to do what it is expected to do. Leaders of people might find their followers could benefit from being treated in a similar manner. How many times have you assigned your employees a task, taken only a minute or two to prepare them and then left them on their own?

How many times did they come to you to complain that they are not sure if they are doing the right thing – let alone doing it the right way? Or worse, they plug ahead and do a mediocre job, at best. Then the work has to be redone, resulting in a waste of time and effort. No one is happy, and it could even result in employees *not* coming to you for guidance since they want to avoid your displeasure.

However, what if we took a lesson from how we teach a new task to a dog? What if the first thing the leader did was to grasp the big picture. Suppose he started with a vision of what a perfect performance would look like.

With an understanding of the task to be completed, the effective leader could ensure that:

- The employee knew the steps involved in completing the task
- Recognized how long it might take to learn and complete each step
- Understood how to combine the steps into one smooth operation to create the desired "product," and throughout the entire process the leader
- Demonstrated he knew how to motivate the employee.

Creating a Motivating Work Environment

The lesson here is best illustrated by the first of the three characteristics that define a *Motivating Work Environment.*

Characteristic #1 requires the leader to ensure that a mutually determined view of work goals (expectations) exists and a mutually determined view of what constitutes a job well done is understood.

This can be done easily enough in the workplace. All it takes is two people, a supervisor and an employee, two chairs, maybe a couple of cups of coffee, and the willingness to talk to one another.

With dogs, it's a little more difficult. It's impractical to suggest that owners and their dogs sit down over a cup of coffee and come to an understanding of "expectations" or what constitutes a "job well done." However, that must be accomplished if the "task" is to be completed correctly.

Therefore, dog trainers know that, regardless of the circumstances, they have a responsibility to be clear and understandable when communicating their expectations to their dogs. They also know they can only do that if they understand the need for, and the importance of, setting high, but achievable, goals, not only for the dog but also for themselves.

Should it be any different in the workplace? Once again, there is an important lesson here for people who manage the activities of others. Without exception, the need to set high expectations is paramount in a high-performance organization. Mediocre expectations produce mediocre results.

Here's an example of how a dog trainer approaches "expectations." First of all, in dog training, we know that it is just as easy to do an exercise correctly as it is to turn in a substandard performance.

Consider the simple act of sitting. Dogs are supposed to sit on their haunches, not side-ways on their hips. It takes no more effort to perform a perfect sit than it does to do a "sloppy sit." Trainers, therefore, are instructed not to let the dog choose how the sit is to be done. They are to set a high expectation level. In fact, it should be perfect! Teach dogs to do this exercise correctly, never let them get away with doing it incorrectly, and they will only learn how to do it right.

To summarize, whether working with dogs, or with people, we are talking about establishing:

1. An understanding of what is expected; and
2. That what is expected represents very high standards.

Works for dogs. Works for people!

All of this information has to be conveyed to a dog (or a person). How is that done? We call it the communication process. Ah, the communications process - such an easy thing to master.

The 5th Leadership Lesson Learned in Dog Obedience School

Dog trainers and leaders both need to grasp the big picture. They need to know what a perfect performance looks like and understand the steps that need to be mastered that will result in a perfect performance. With an understanding of the task to be completed, they:

- can communicate the steps required to complete the task
- know how long it might take to learn or complete each step
- know how to combine the steps into one smooth operation, and throughout the process
- demonstrate that they know how to motivate the employee.

Chapter 11

Prosper by Learning How to Talk to a Dog

Communicating with people is not an easy process. Enter most any workplace and chances are you will hear those famous nine words. "What we have here is a failure to communicate."

Successfully conveying information to others is fraught with challenges. Barriers exist everywhere. The words we choose, the sender or receiver's attitude, and our tone of voice are three common barriers. Considering all the things that can go wrong, it's a wonder that any message is sent *or* received accurately.

Most of us understand the importance of effective communication skills. Leaders certainly do. Consider for a moment a few of the characteristics associated with leaders. They are people who influence the actions of others, are effective in getting people to accept their ideas, and they provide guidance and direction. They have a *vision* of how things could be. They are focused on that vision, and they have the ability to make it "real" to others. So real, in fact, they inspire others to pursue that dream.

And, how do they accomplish all of this? By being outstanding communicators. They have harnessed the power of the spoken and written word. Without the ability to communicate their vision, dreams and ideas, why would anybody choose to listen to them?

Ironically, things are no different in the dog obedience ring. The trainer must be able to convey to the dog his or her image of the perfect performance. The trainer has to overcome the language differences that exist between the species and make themselves understood in spite of the barriers that exist. Poor communicators make poor dog trainers.

The Communication Process

Since we are dealing with the subject of communication skills, a definition of communication is required. Ask most people how they define communication, and they will probably say something along the lines of "It's an exchange of information between two or more people." However, it is much more than that. The best definition of communication I know defines it as follows:

"Communication is the process by which information is exchanged and through which all human relationships are formed or changed.

It is the means by which all human motivation is guided toward organized, productive effort."

Think about that for a moment. It is important we understand the depth of the term "communication." It's more than simply conveying information. It's the process by which can we can change someone's behavior.

As for the actual process, it requires a sender, a receiver, a means for transferring information and, hopefully, feedback. Feedback tells us whether our messages were received as we intended. It tells us something about the receiver's attitude, and we use it to impose or change behaviors. Think of "feedback" as answering the question: "What is the effect" of the message. Feedback is an essential ingredient of two-way communication.

The process is illustrated as follows:

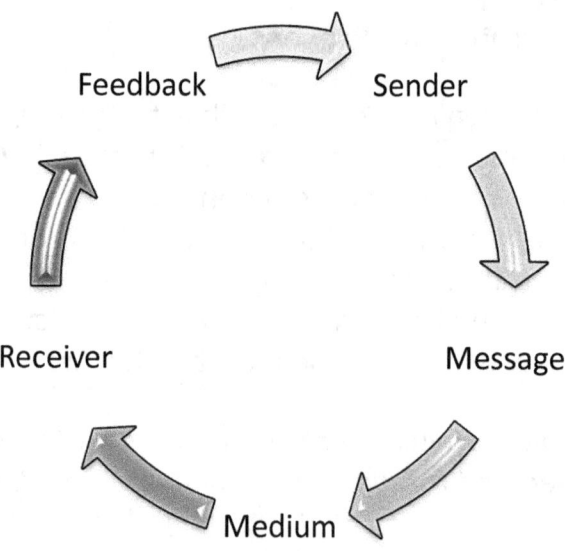

What We Can Learn From Communicating With a Dog

Whether communicating with dogs or people, the process is the same. However, consider how much more difficult it is to convey a message to a dog. You can tell a person to pay attention or to look you in the eye. You cannot do that with a dog. Yet, making that connection is essential if the dog is to learn anything. If you cannot establish this "communication link," you will be forever talking to a furry skin that doesn't acknowledge your existence.

When communicating with people, research has shown there are three factors that influence a receiver's understanding and perception of a message. They are:

- The words used (the verbal aspect of the message),
- The body language, (the non-verbal aspect), and
- Paralanguage, which refers to the speaker's rate of speech, tone and pitch of the voice.

When communicating with a dog, trainers are concerned with these same aspects. However, the first thing a trainer has to do is *get* the dog's attention. After that, they have to know how to talk to the dog so it doesn't tune them out. People-to-people communication offers the same challenge.

In a training class, we demonstrate that, to a dog, the words we use mean little if anything. You can call your dog every name in the book, but if you use a happy, enthusiastic tone of voice, the dog will think you're wonderful. As long as you *sound* happy, they will respond in a positive way.

Some people have taken this a step further by substituting nonsense words for commonly used commands. They might teach their dog to "sit" by telling it to "speak." Or, they might teach their dog to respond to commands given in another language. I'm probably not the only person who knows someone who thought it would be cute to teach their German Shepherd to respond to commands given in German.

Think of the possibilities. Wouldn't it be fun to learn to speak some ancient, cryptic, language? No one but you and your dog would know what you were talking about. Wait a minute. I think that has already been done in the workplace. We call it every day boss-to-employee communication. And to further exacerbate the situation, we use acronyms, tech-speak and other ways of making sure no one knows what the heck we're talking about!

Proper Voice Control

With dogs, we focus on the "paralanguage" aspect. What is important *is how* we say *what* we say. Trainers learn that when they talk to their dogs, there are three "voices" they can use. Depending on the situation, they have to use the most appropriate voice.

Used most often is the *encouraging voice*. Such a voice would be very enthusiastic, with plenty of words of praise. For example, imagine the owner of the puppy calling for the dog to "*come.*" The dog may have no idea what the word "come" means. However, it hears a voice that is happy, maybe at a higher pitch then the normal speaking voice it is used to hearing. The owner's body language reflects a positive tone – arms open, hands clapping. The dog hearing this *"voice"* usually responds by running to the owner, tail wagging and offering lots of puppy kisses.

I've often thought this would be an effective voice for managers to use to get a positive response from an employee. But then the idea of a manager using such an enthusiastic voice, with plenty of words of encouragement and praise (while clapping his hands) would probably get him arrested.

The second voice the trainer learns to use is the *command voice*. This is nothing more than their normal speaking voice. We use this voice all the time. "Take out the garbage." "Close the door." Wash the dishes." If someone asks you to do any of these items in a polite but directive way, they are using their command voice. With a dog, telling it to "Sit" or "Come" in a normal speaking voice with just a *hint* of an order to comply would be a typical example of using a commanding voice.

Then we have the *demanding voice.* This voice is used for those times when the dog knows what it is supposed to do, but doesn't do it when commanded. It hears the command but decides you can't possibly be serious about such a ridiculous request. Therefore, the command is given with a greater sense of authority.

There is a fourth voice. One that trainers are instructed never to use. For lack of a better term, I'll call it the *out of control voice*. It probably doesn't need further clarification. Losing one's temper and shouting has never been an effective training (or management) technique.

Communicating with people is no less challenging. I am amazed (and amused) at how some people talk to one another. Like dogs, it is interesting to see their hackles go up if they think there is even the slightest hint of a threat.

Using the right "voice" at the right time is a useful lesson, and is a powerful leadership tool when used correctly.

In One Ear and Out the Other

People, and dogs, can be poor listeners. When people do not listen, they only hear what they want to hear or what they expect to hear. For example, if all they hear is criticism, they will only expect to hear more criticism. They will always be on the defensive and if, by some miracle, there is "good news," they will not "hear" it.

© **Klara Viskova - Fotolia.com**

Further, we should recognize people hear what they been *conditioned* to hear. Suppose your boss is a micro-manager who calls you every day to tell you the exact same thing. Day after day after day. After a couple of weeks, should the message change, you may not hear it because you have tuned him out. You have been conditioned to hear just one message, and that's the only message you hear.

Dogs are not very different. Yell at your dog for every little thing it does wrong (in your opinion), and chances are you will only see more problems. It is very disheartening to see a dog's attitude go from happy to defensive when it hears its owner's voice. We often see this same reaction in the workplace. Watch people in an office scramble to look busy or try to become *"invisible"* when they hear the voice of their supervisor. They, too, can quickly go from happy to defensive if all they hear is criticism or insults.

When it comes to listening, dogs are quite capable of tuning people out if they don't approve of the messages they are hearing. They are experts at what we call "selective listening." Selective listing is similar to hearing only what you want to hear. Many an owner has experienced this phenomenon. When they call for their dog to "come" with the intention of giving it a bath, the dog shows all the signs of "sudden deafness syndrome." On the other hand, if they drop a dog biscuit onto a plush carpet on the other side of the house, the dog comes running.

When instructing a training course, it is interesting to watch the lines of communication develop between the handler and dog. When the dog's attention is focused on the trainer, when their eyes meet, you know they have connected.

In spite of what the majority of people think, few of them are effective communicators. If only people would recognize the problems created due to their poor or non-existent communication skills. How much more effective and productive would they be if they actually heard what was being said?

Do you want to become a better communicator? Learn how to "talk" and "listen" to a dog. Prove you have the ability to communicate clearly and effectively in a way that even a dog would understand. Do that well, and you *will* improve your ability to communicate with people.

The 6th Leadership Lesson Learned in Dog Obedience School

You are not as effective at communicating your thoughts and ideas as you think. You can improve your communication skills by learning to listen. Listen well and you may hear something you can use.

Your tone of voice can have a dramatic impact on people. Dog trainers learn that when they talk to their dogs there are three "voices" they can use. Depending on the situation, they are to use the appropriate voice to get positive results. The same goes for leaders.

Develop the patience and skills necessary to communicate with a dog and you will improve your ability to communicate with people. Communication skills are essential to conveying information and shaping behaviors. Without the ability to communicate effectively, nothing can become operational.

The 7th Leadership Lesson Learned in Dog Obedience School

Setting expectations is important for both the trainer and the trainee. When setting expectations, you are attempting to do accomplish two objectives:

- communicate an understanding of what is expected, and
- that what is expected represents very high standards

Chapter 12

How and When to Praise

How and When to Correct

Newspapers are for Reading – not for Whacking.

On occasion, I would have the opportunity to visit a training class conducted by an instructor whose techniques were, shall we say, a bit primitive. A common practice would be to have the novice handlers drag their dogs onto the training floor before either of them had learned anything. Since no one had a clue what they were supposed to do, their dogs would be jerked all over the place. It was obvious no one was learning a thing. The dogs weren't very happy, and neither were the owners.

Over the years, I've encountered similar situations in many work environments where managers, whose techniques were, shall we say, a bit primitive, would jerk their people all around the office floor. Again, it was obvious no one was learning a thing.

Such behavior should be unacceptable in either environment though it is easier to control in an obedience class. After all, the message the majority of obedience instructors are trying to convey is that the students have enrolled in an "obedience" training class, not a "submission-training" class.

Of course, I am not suggesting people be obedient in the same manner as we expect a dog to be. Leaders do not want an office full of people who sit around waiting to be told what to do next. They do not want a staff of robots who cannot think or lack the initiative to do their jobs unless specifically told what, when, where or how to do it.

What they want are willing workers who are up to the challenges they face, who know what is expected of them and who can make intelligent decisions.

Maybe it would be appropriate to think about substituting the word *motivated* for *obedient*. Enlighten leaders know the advantages of creating a motivating work environment. Earlier I presented characteristic #1 of a motivating work environment. It stated that leaders must take steps to ensure that a mutually determined view of work goals (expectations) exists and a mutually determined view of what constitutes a job well done is understood.

Presented here are characteristics #2 and #3 of a Motivating Work Environment. They are:

- A supportive, not coercive, environment, and
- Providing reinforcement, appreciation and recognition for a job well done

Incorporating these characteristics into the way you lead requires an understanding of behavior modification, operant conditioning and a huge dose of common sense.

Unfortunately, to quote Voltaire, "Common sense is not so common."

Praising people for a job well done is one of the characteristics of an effective leader. The only problem is, it seems like no one receives praise for a well-done job! One of the questions I ask people during seminars is, "How many of you have received praise or some form of positive feedback from someone other than your peers anytime in the past six months?" I'm lucky if one out of ten people responds with "Me!"

I then ask how many of them take the time to provide positive feedback to their employees when they catch them doing something right. The odds improve a little, with maybe three in 10 replying, "I do." Still not the numbers one would hope to see.

Once again, anyone thinking about leading people should take a cue from a dog trainer. Dog trainers know to praise their dog for everything it does right and even to praise it when it *does nothing wrong*. They do this, and they get outstanding results.

Novice trainers learn they are only to discipline their dog when circumstances require it, and only when a number of criteria have been met. In fact, during the first training session, they do not learn techniques for redirecting inappropriate behavior except for serious infractions of proper dog etiquette.

Why? Because at this stage the dog doesn't have a clue what you want it to do. You are in the *Telling* stage. You talk, they listen. At this point, there is nothing to correct.

How and When to Praise

The question comes down to how and when to praise. Ken Blanchard, the co-author of numerous books on creating and maintaining a dynamic workplace, wrote in <u>The One Minute Manager</u> that managers should "*Catch people doing things right*." Dog trainers have been doing this for years, except their philosophy has been:

"Catch Your Dog Doing It Right!"

When you begin to catch people (or a dog) doing things right, and then praise them and let them know you've noticed their good performance, their attention (or your dog's attention) perks up.

Providing Rewards that Mean Something

It is critical to keep in mind that the type of praise heaped upon the employee is an important consideration. A fundamental concept of dog training is not all dogs respond to the same reward. Offer one dog a fuzzy toy mouse, and it will be in heaven. Offer it to another, and it may not even give it a second look. Trainers know that when they provide the dog a reward, it must mean something. The reward could be a special toy or food item. Whatever it is, the dog must see it as something special – something worth the effort.

Over 60 years ago, B. F. Skinner presented his theories on behavior modification. He based his system on operant conditioning. By definition, operant conditioning means, *"a behavior is followed by a consequence, and the type of consequence modifies the organisms' tendency to repeat the behavior in the future."* Briefly, he proposed that:

- A behavior followed by a reinforcing stimulus results in an increased probability of that behavior occurring in the future.
- A behavior no longer followed by the reinforcing stimulus results in a decreased probability of that behavior occurring in the future.

He also provided insight into how best to provide rewards. Thanks to Skinner, here is what we know about rewarding people:

- Rewards that are specific are best. They should mean something to the "rewardee."
- The best rewards are those that are given immediately.
- They are spontaneous.
- They should be sincere.

Regarding the issue of sincerity. People can tell when you are faking it! Someone once called insincere praise the "skunk factor" because employees know something doesn't smell right.

Building on the idea that rewards should be specific and that the best rewards are those that are given immediately when working with a dog, we use a training technique called "shaping" that employs these same attributes.

Shaping is the process by which you gradually teach a dog a new action or behavior by rewarding it during each step of the process while learning that behavior. Of course, you would have to break the exercise down into its individual parts to be successful with this technique. But, if you do, a potentially complicated action can become one that your dog will learn and understand more quickly.

While catching behavior is a good training method when teaching a dog behaviors he does naturally like sitting, laying down, etc., *shaping* is more effective in teaching a dog more unnatural actions and behaviors such as fetching, running an agility course, etc. Its important for the trainer to provide the dog with a reward at the right time coupled with a simple word like "Yes" to reinforce that what the dog just did was the desired behavior.

Without getting into the step-by-step process used with our dogs, imagine if we used such a process when teaching an employee a new task. I can see it now; the supervisor would have a little pouch attached to his or her waist filled with a suitable reward. Something like chocolate or doughnut holes. And, when the employee performs a task correctly, the employee is offered a reward along with the word "Yes!".

Positive reinforcement is central to every successful dog trainer's success. Operant conditioning is the centerpiece of today's dog training philosophy. If you want to become an expert on positive reinforcement, don't read books written by people about people. Read books written by people about dogs.

How and When to Discipline

How and when do you discipline? Well, certainly not with the frequency and in the way most people do. How would you react if every time your boss wanted to get a point across he or she hit you with a rolled-up newspaper? Or, suppose you weren't sure what was expected of you, and the only way you knew you did something right was that you weren't hit (this time).

It's like housebreaking a dog. What do people do when they come home and in the middle of their white carpet, is an unwelcome gift left by the dog? They might rant and rave, yelling at the dog about its indiscretion.

What is the dog thinking? It's thinking that its owner, the love of its life, just walked in the door and is mad at him or her for simply being there.

When someone is in the process of housing-breaking their dog, they learn that rubbing their dog's nose in a wet spot, if not done at the moment of the indiscretion, only teaches the dog not to rub its nose in a wet spot. More than likely the dog already knows that!

Trainers have a term for this type of correction. It's called *after-the-fact discipline*. It is not an effective way to correct undesirable behaviors such as chewing on your new Nikes or soiling the carpet when the owner is absent or unaware. The informed dog owner knows they need to correct mistakes when they happen or when the performance is not at the level desired, not months later at the dog's annual performance evaluation.

Neither is it an effective way to redirect inappropriate behavior in people. Waiting months until an annual performance review, or simply ignoring a less than adequate job performance, does nothing to improve performance. Dog trainers know this, and they practice it.

Managers should be so wise.

The 8th Leadership Lesson Learned in Dog Obedience School

Rewarding your dog is not the same as occasionally tossing it a bone to keep it happy (or to keep it from biting you!).

Dogs or People - rewards must mean something to the recipients and they must be applied immediately to be effective.

Correct mistakes when they happen (or when the performance is not at the desired level), not months later at the dog's annual performance evaluation.

The 9th Leadership Lesson Learned in Dog Obedience School

Whether telling a dog or an employee that it has performed a "job well-done", effective leaders:

- *Praise often*
- *Praise sincerely*
- *Praise as if they mean it!*

They know:

- Behaviors or actions that are rewarded or recognized are repeated
- Inappropriate and undesirable behaviors that are ignored are repeated

Chapter 13

Situational Leadership® for Dog Trainers

Dogs, like people, will challenge you to use a style of leadership that fits the current situation. Effective trainers know how and when to "tailor" their style in order to influence and modify the behavior of their dogs. They may not be aware of it, but the process they use to select the most appropriate *style* mirrors the principles of Situational Leadership®.

As previously stated, Situational Leadership® is a model

of leadership co-developed in 1969 by Dr. Paul Hersey and Dr. Ken Blanchard. Taught to thousands of managers in every conceivable type of business environment, this model has become the basis of the most prevalent leadership system in the world.

There are three terms you need to be familiar with to understand how Situational Leadership® works. They are:

1. **Task behavior,** which refers to the extent the leader spells out who will do what, when, where and how.

2. **Relationship behavior,** which refers to the extent the leader engages in behaviors such as listening, encouraging, coaching or providing socio-emotional support, and

3. **Readiness level,** which is defined as to how ready, willing and able someone is to do the job he or she is expected to do.

Situational Leadership® requires the leader to adjust his or her leadership style based on the employee's readiness level. The entire process is based on an interplay between:

- The amount of task behavior engaged in by the leader.
- The amount of relationship behavior the leader provides; and
- The readiness level the followers demonstrate in performing a specific task or activity.

Whether dealing with dogs or people, the major challenge is to accurately evaluate an individual's readiness level, as it determines the amount of task and relationship behaviors the leader should engage in.

Situational Leadership® presents the manager with four styles of leadership to choose from depending on the current situation. The four styles and examples of when applying each style would be most appropriate, follows:

Style 1: Telling or Directing. In the workplace, this style would be appropriate when teaching someone a new task. Its equivalent in the dog world would be a situation where you were trying to teach your dog a new trick. The dog has no idea what it is you want it to do. Therefore, it's trainer (leader) directed. You talk, the dog listens.

Style 2: Selling or Coaching. This style is used when encouragement is needed. For example, it would be appropriate when someone is practicing the skills or tasks they have been taught.

For the dog trainer, he might use this style after the dog knows what is required of it, but the dog still needs lots of encouragement. Here's where you'll hear lots of words of encouragement such as "Good Dog," "Way to go" and so on.

Style 3: Participating or Supporting. This style is exemplified by a teamwork approach to resolving an issue. While the leader still provides guidance, the employee exercises greater control over their job assignments and provides input into accomplishing those tasks.

You've seen this style in action if you've ever watched a herding dog exhibition. At such events, one of the herding breeds, usually a Border Collie, works with its human counterpart to bring a flock of sheep (or sometimes geese or ducks) into a pen. The human partner provides directions to the dog who must execute those commands, sometimes at a far distance. Making the most of interspecies communication, such teams epitomize the working relationship between man and dog that has fostered livestock farming for hundreds of years.

Style 4: Delegating. At this level, you would have employees who know what to do, how to do it and can get things done without any direct supervision. They are ready, willing and able to do their job.

In the dog world, I naturally think of working livestock guardian dogs. Here you have a dog that has been left alone with hundreds of sheep, and it has the awesome responsibility of protecting those sheep from all sorts of predators. If there are humans in the vicinity, the dog must make a distinction between friend or foe and react accordingly. They can't wait for their owner to tell them to spring into action. They have to make decisions on the correct course of action. A failure to act means certain death to its flock. They are ready, willing and able to do their job.

Training an Employee Like You Train a Dog

In the workplace, unless we are dealing with a leader who understands how to identify these needs, the most likely scenario goes something like this - the employee is told once how to do something and then is expected to flawlessly perform that duty forever.

Imagine doing the same thing to a dog. Suppose you're a dog and all week long, you're free to run around, play, explore and do doggie stuff.

However, once a week someone puts a collar around your neck. The collar is attached to a leash. The person holding the leash then demands you perform a series of tasks you have not been properly trained to do. Not that it matters. You're expected to do them anyway.

If you react too slowly, you receive "a slight correction." If you walk a little too slowly and lag behind this person, you receive another "slight correction." Sit too slow, get up too soon or look away at the wrong moment, and *zap*, receive another "slight correction."

How many of you would be a willing worker, excited to move through your paces, if you were treated in such a manner? Do you think you might constantly be on guard, tensing your neck muscles as you await the next "jerk" (as in the name of the person holding the other end of the leash)?

More than likely, you would be afraid to do anything because you would never be sure if what you were doing was the right thing. Moreover, you know doing the wrong thing would result in your head being separated from your shoulders.

What do dogs do when this happens? They sit there with their neck muscles tensed up, and they do not move until they are pushed or pulled into the position the leash-holder wants. They are constantly on the defensive. They are darned if they do and darned if they don't.

Isn't that exactly what some managers do? There's a name for this type of management. Ken Blanchard, the author of the *One Minute Manager* series, referred to it as the Leave Alone/Zap School of Management. It is characterized by managers who leave their people alone to try to figure out how to complete a task. If things are done correctly, no feedback is provided. However, if a mistake is made, zap, they've got you!

Like the dog who just sits there with its neck muscles tensed up refusing to move, employees will just sit there until told exactly what to do. They are constantly on the defensive. They are darned if they do, and darned if they don't.

Knowledgeable trainers know they need to flex their "style" to suit each situation. A new task requires a different style than a task that is "old hat." Of course, an old task that is no longer being done correctly also requires a change in style.

I think it is clear. Before anyone is allowed to assume the duties and responsibilities associated with a supervisory position they should be required to either:

+ Complete a dog obedience training course, or
+ Complete a Situational Leadership® workshop, or
+ Complete both

The odds of them becoming the type of supervisor most of us only dream about would greatly increase.

The 10th Leadership Lesson Learned in Dog Obedience School

If we want to obtain the highest quality performance from our dogs, we need to treat them in a way that brings out the best performance. A simple statement but it requires true leadership skills to accomplish.

To accomplish this goal, trainers must understand the lessons learned from Situational Leadership® and apply those lessons to creating motivated performers.

Chapter 14

"Exercise Over. Praise Your Dog"

An obedience class instructor will use the words "Exercise over. Praise your dog" after guiding the dogs and trainers through a task. It's a reminder to the trainers to reinforce the dog's good performance so as to increase the likelihood of a repeat of that performance. It would not be a bad idea if leaders in the workplace also put into practice the idea of rewarding a good performance to

 increase the likelihood of seeing a repeat of that performance.

What we know about motivating and rewarding dogs closely parallels what leaders know about motivating and rewarding people. The rewards we offer dogs may be different, but the philosophy that dictates how and when we reward is the same.

After instructing numerous dog obedience training courses, I have concluded that everyone who tries hard enough can successfully train their dog. If they work at it, and they apply the lessons they have been taught, most everyone can mold a dog into an enthusiastic, motivated and "willing-worker."

I would estimate that when dogs fail to learn, in almost every instance, the reasons are the same as the ones we encounter when we see performance problems in people:

1. the manager did something wrong to the employee, or
2. the manager failed to do something right for the employee

You might want to reread those two statements. They contain a great deal of truth. I believe it was Dr. Deming who concluded that somewhere in the neighborhood of 85% of the performance problems we see in employees are the result of something the manager did or didn't do.

There are four little "training truths" I pass along to people working with their dogs. These truths apply just as much to people.

1. The quality of the performance is not based solely on how energetic and enthusiastic your dog is. The most enthusiastic dog may not necessarily be the smartest or the quickest to learn. How the dog is "led" is what makes the difference.

2. Many a happy dog, through poor management, has turned into a less than satisfactory performer.

3. Many dogs with less than desired levels of enthusiasm have blossomed into outstanding performers because of the leadership skills of the trainer.

4. Moreover, many dogs have succeeded in spite of their trainers. They rise above the shortcomings of their trainers.

Just like people, some dogs will always perform slightly better, slightly faster and with slightly more enthusiasm than others.

As a dog trainer, I know that if I want to obtain the highest quality performance from my dog, I need to treat him/her in a way that brings out the best performance. Such a simple statement, yet one that requires considerable skills to achieve. I also know I cannot expect or demand the dog's loyalty and trust. That has to be earned through words, behaviors and actions.

At the end of Chapter 3, I wrote that we are not born with some innate ability to train a dog any more than we are born with the qualities, skills or knowledge that make us a leader of people. How we learn and develop those skills is up to us, and I mentioned there are many ways to pursue a personal "degree" in leadership.

I still believe that anyone who desires to lead people should first be required to demonstrate that he or she has the patience and understanding to train a dog. Throughout the training, their dog would have to remain animated and motivated. Two-way communication would have to be established and be evident in the way the dog and trainer interact.

Only after the trainer demonstrates that he or she can successfully "lead" a dog would they be allowed to lead people.

However, then I think about some of the managers and supervisors I have known, and I wonder just how fair that would be to the dog.

How or where you learn your leadership lessons is not important. To repeat what was written earlier in the book: attend workshops, read books, watch videos. It doesn't matter how you go about it – just "go about it"!

The results will be employees who make you and your organization **High in Trial** winners, not just another pack of runner-ups.

Chapter 15

Summary

Summarized below are the first ten leadership lessons learned in dog obedience school:

Lesson 1:

The first training class is no different than the first day on a new job or in a new position. Each subsequent class is designed to enhance the dog's performance further. When combined, all the classes can be considered the equivalent of a new employee orientation program.

A well-developed and thought-out orientation program should have two phases. Phase 1 spans the first day through the first week of employment. The focus is on setting expectations and explaining goals and objectives.

Phase 2 is an extended training phase and might last as long as six months to a year. It is during this time that organizations should take steps to integrate the employee into the culture and philosophy of how work is done in the organization.

An orientation program provides employees with an opportunity to develop a firm foundation upon which all subsequent growth is based. It helps avoid mass confusion and sets the stage for future growth and development. It doesn't matter whether we are referring to a dog-training class or the corporate environment; providing a well-thought-out orientation program is a necessity.

In summary, it should be more than showing the dog the location of the nearest restroom (tree).

Lesson #2

Watch for signs you are dealing with "ring-wise employees." Such workers know how, and what, they are supposed to do. They just don't want to do it! They will test you on a regular basis to see how serious you are about them doing the work assigned to them.

Additionally, leaders must be able to differentiate between a "training problem" and a "performance problem." Knowing the difference allows you to provide an appropriate response to redirecting the undesired performance.

Lesson #3

Dogs are trained using a leash and collar. Think of employees as having imaginary ones. Dog trainers know they must master the art of leash control. So must leaders. Both must learn how and when to give their people some slack, or when to reel them in.

Where dogs are concerned, their slip collars can become choke collars if used improperly. Where people are concerned, improper usage of their imaginary collars can, and will, "choke" off initiative and undermine motivation.

Lesson #4

Every dog is different. Every employee is different. To train your dog, or prepare your people, you need to know them. To motivate, teach and lead them you need the insight to recognize what works and what doesn't. Know this, and you will be able to select the most appropriate course of action from a multitude of possible actions for every situation. It's a lesson that works equally as well with people.

To effectively mold and mentor dogs or people, you must learn:

- How they "think" or processes information
- How fast a learner they are
- How they respond to praise or corrections
- The best way to motivate them
- How much guidance and direction they need
- How much patience you will need to guide either of them to the level of performance desired.

Lesson #5

You are not as effective at communicating your thoughts and ideas as you think. You can improve your communication skills by learning to listen. Listen well, and you may hear something you can use.

Your tone of voice can have a dramatic impact on people. Dog trainers learn that when they talk to their dogs, there are three "voices" they can use. Depending on the situation, they are to use the appropriate voice to get positive results. The same goes for leaders.

Develop the patience and skills necessary to communicate with a dog, and you will improve your ability to communicate with people. Communication skills are essential to conveying information and shaping behaviors. Without the ability to communicate effectively, nothing can become operational.

Lesson #6

Dog trainers and leaders both need to grasp the big picture. They need to have a vision of what a perfect performance looks like, and understand the steps that must be mastered to turn in that perfect performance.

With an understanding of the tasks to be completed they:

- can communicate the steps required to complete the task
- know how long it might take to learn or complete each step

- know how to combine the steps into one smooth operation, and throughout the process
- demonstrate that they know how to motivate the employee

Lesson #7

Setting expectations is important for both the trainer and the trainee. Whether working with dogs or with people, when setting expectations you are attempting to convey the following:

1. An understanding of what is expected, and
2. That what is expected represents very high standards.

Lesson #8

Rewarding your dog is not the same as occasionally tossing it a bone to keep it happy (or to keep it from biting you!).

Correct mistakes when they happen (or when the performance is not at the desired level), not months later at the dog's annual performance evaluation.

And, when rewarding an outstanding performance for dogs or people, remember that rewards must mean something to the recipient, and they must be applied immediately to be effective.

Lesson #9

Whether telling a dog or an employee that it has performed a "job well-done," effective leaders:

- Praise often
- Praise sincerely
- Praise as if they mean it!

They know:

- Behaviors or actions that are rewarded or recognized are repeated
- Inappropriate and undesirable behaviors that are ignored are repeated

Lesson #10

If we want to obtain the highest quality performance from our dogs, we need to treat them in a way that brings out the best performance. A simple statement but it requires true leadership skills to accomplish.

To accomplish this goal, trainers must understand the lessons learned from Situational Leadership® and apply those lessons to create motivated performers.

Chapter 16

The Leadership Lessons Learned in Cat Obedience School

The End

About the Author

Combining lessons learned from training dogs with lessons learned from training people, Doug offers a unique approach to personal and professional development training programs.

When not conducting workshops on a variety of interpersonal development programs, Doug Young lives on a small farm with a menagerie of animals, including Anatolian Shepherd dogs and Dandie Dinmont Terriers.

Computers are also a passion of Doug and he enjoys spending time maintaining websites for his variety of interests.

You can learn more about any of the above by visiting these websites:

Professional Development Training
> www.thecanineway.com

Dandie Dinmont Terriers
> www.montizard.com

For additional Information contact the author at:

Douglas Young
PO Box 151
Rushville, Ohio 43150
Website: www.thecanineway.com
Email: young@thecanineway.com

Presentation Opportunities

Leadership Lessons Learned in Dog Obedience School

Learn the leadership lessons 1000's of dog obedience school graduates have learned. However, this time, apply this knowledge to create motivated and productive employees.

Leadership Lessons Learned in Dog Obedience School takes a fun but informative look at the skills required to be an effective leader, and answers the tough leadership question, "What would a dog do?"

While we should not treat employees like dogs, we can learn a great deal about creating a motivating work environment by applying dog training lessons to the workplace. Treating a dog right - treating a person right - there's not much difference.

Understanding Personality Styles - The Canine Way.

Learn how your "behavioral preferences" influence your preferred style of leadership. An understanding of this well-researched topic is critical to the success of anyone seeking to assume a leadership role. Our preferred "style" affects how effectively we interact with others. And, knowledge of this topic can help us understand why we prefer one supervisory style over another.

www.ingramcontent.com/pod-product-compliance
Lightning Source LLC
Chambersburg PA
CBHW052328220526
45472CB00001B/324